A Magnificent Loneliness

Also by Allison Benis White

A Magnificent Loneliness

Allison Benis White

Four Way Books
Tribeca

Library of Congress Cataloging-in-Publication Data

Names: White, Allison Benis, 1972– author.
Title: A magnificent loneliness / Allison Benis White.
Description: Tribeca : Four Way Books, 2025.
Identifiers: LCCN 2024035157 (print) | LCCN 2024035158 (ebook) |
ISBN   9781961897229 (trade paperback) | ISBN 9781961897236 (ebook)
Subjects: LCGFT: Poetry.
Classification: LCC PS3623.H569 M34 2025 (print) | LCC PS3623.H569
(ebook) | DDC 811/.6--dc23/eng/20240823
LC record available at https://lccn.loc.gov/2024035157
LC ebook record available at https://lccn.loc.gov/2024035158

This book is manufactured in the United States of America and printed on
acid-free paper.

Four Way Books is a not-for-profit literary press. We are grateful for the assistance
we receive from individual donors, public arts agencies, and private foundations
including the NEA, and the New York State Council on the Arts, a state agency.

We are a proud member of the Community of Literary Magazines and Presses.

Contents

Notes

For a long time I have hoped for better days, but alas, today it is necessary for me to lose all hope. My poor wife suffers more and more. I do not think it is possible to be any weaker.

Claude Monet on his wife, and subject of his paintings,

Camille Monet (1847–1879)

We have art in order not to die of the truth.

Friedrich Nietzsche

For beloveds

Molly Brodak (1980–2020)

René Genovese (1978–2021)

Batyah White (1951–2021)

The Woman in a Green Dress

after Claude Monet, oil on canvas, 1866

What if I devoted myself

        to a wave of black and green — floor-length, mid-crash

filling my mind? To survive. Bear with me. On seeing

       Monet's *The Woman in a Green Dress* for the first

time, Emile Zola wrote, "Just

        consider that dress . . . softly it drags, it is alive."

As if leaving was a religion,

she is turning away, and turning her head back

to allow us to see her leaving—to conceive

her train of black and green. I don't know how to see

the world but not to see. How to love the world but to see

one thing completely.

Or to come to the end of seeing.

I want to look at her forever. To finish myself, I thought,

                                        on my walk, watching the green

parrots huddled in the branches of the evergreens, almost

invisible but for the shaking of the leaves.

Mostly black with a sliver of green,

                    I found a parrot feather on the sidewalk

near the trees, dragged it across my lips. This is the truth, I thought,

        pay attention. I remember

once, turning to leave, a black purse over her shoulder, a black purse

over her living shoulder, Love said   nothing to me.

Bear with me — my eyes are alive with it.

As with the parrots, sometimes hundreds, mostly green, screeching in the trees.

To hold still, or finish myself.

When I'm tired of seeing, and therefore entirely, I would like to lie down in Bremen,

Germany, in front of the painting and sleep.

Love does not love thee.

I remember. On seeing *The Woman in a Green Dress* for the first time,

Theophile Thoré wrote, "a standing woman seen

from behind trailing a magnificent green silk dress—"

A magnificent loneliness.

This is all I want to say

       about my life. When I picked up the feather,

 I thought of her dress. I don't know

           how to love the world but to confess. I remember,

       as a child, before the light turned green,

knowing I did not know

(a first memory)

the woman in the next car, and she did not know me.

Consider her profile, looking down, fingers curled to her face.

If this is the world, more reaching than seeing,   what I'm doing

        with my eyes: her black and green

stripes. All my life, I thought, if I could make something

alive. Only later, I thought, to look
                                me in the eye.

Entirely—to finish myself.

                              Like a portrait. Bear with me.
The solid black background

              was used to keep the focus

on her dress, to see the train

more clearly. I don't know how to love   the world but to love

              her leaving. How to leave

                        the world but to turn to leave her—

              but to turn my head back

         to see her.

Postcards to M.

for Molly

That you have grown still enough to write to.

Or to be left alone—to be left alone.

A few hours from here, a field of poppies so red I want to be cut.

Stain the seams, tear myself apart.

That place so close to the end of a song.

In the pause, just afterward, the silence rushing in.

Here is my mind, here is my mind (tilted into my hands).

What kind of loneliness is this, kissing every finger?

To your lost room: all pictures of wildflowers.

To your lost room: honey poured on your tongue by someone you love.

Silence, thick as frosting, in my mouth.

Then the music of your name.

A place to tell you something—to tell myself.

I tried to call you in the dream but I could not dial correctly.

I could not die correctly.

In a dark gold dress, the madness has gone quiet.

A memory of your face as radiant anxiety.

Opening a series of boxes, and inside the last, smallest one, a pearl.

What things did you imagine to cool your mind?

Even if it is to die, it is beautiful to decide.

In the window, my face trapped in light.

A cut-out woman in a cut-out dress, cutting out her paper death.

What is there to feel now that would matter?

Here: wish you were.

Women in the Garden

after Claude Monet, oil on canvas, 1866

for René

What is alive between us?

I am asking with my mouth

to the woman in the white dress

who is running away—arms outstretched as if to greet

someone unseen, left of frame. My subject is

loneliness.

*

My subject is the woman in the white dress

                                    who is running away. Mostly, I am ashamed and amazed.

I am looking at the painting to save my eyes.

                                    *

The women are dead but can be spoken to.

                                    What ended you? What ended you?

                                    A knife, the whiteness of the flowers. Heinrich writes,

"It may be that *Women in the Garden* revealed Monet's subject to him

for the first time: light."

*

The goal of the painting is to see through the painting.

The goal of the painting is to feel your eyes.

I am touching the strange bouquet of the mind,

suicide. "Sunlight," Heinrich writes,

"spread like a great towel on the path."

*

The woman in the white dress is still

running away. Camille Monet

posed for each woman, as I do, as I do. How they all

died and I don't have anywhere to see you.

*

"She seems frozen in her poses," Heinrich writes. And yes, they make no sense

                                        (unbuttoning in the dark, I will come apart

in your mouth, a light nearing honey). Heinrich writes, "the figures

                                        do not seem part of the natural scene." Yes, I am

unnatural here, too.

                                        *

                                        They have come to the garden to take their lives.

Maybe the woman in white is running away

                  to hide behind the trees. Maybe she just wants

privacy. I apologize.

                  I am closing my eyes.

                  *

                  Goodbye, light pouring through the mind,

song of violence, and sounds

that would rather be silence. "For me, the subject

is of secondary importance," Monet wrote,

"I want to convey what is alive

between me and the subject."

*

I have come to the garden to say goodbye.

To kneel before my subject. Yes,

I am taking off my dress to mean *tenderness*.

What is alive between us.

Description of Symptoms

after filling out intake forms for a doctor's appointment

Now my hands buried

in my hair, resting on piano keys

in the back of my head.

This is the music I am playing

through my mind: a dark room singing

a song that will not have children.

Lying on the floor tonight, snowflakes
cut from paper laid over my eyes, a hand
carved from wood laid over my mouth.
If the truth is the thing you must not say,
I will speak for the vase now
as it falls: it is better never
to be at all.

A hand on the back of my head

made of glass, my love, my eyes,

filled with wire, life. Once

I watched a bird's shadow cross a field

in the wind: a black hat that could not stop

tumbling. My eyes are sore

from seeing, my lips from speaking.

How a ribbon curls when pulled

across a scissor's blade—I am practicing

transformation, pain. How the dark hair

of imagination, uncut, grows down

to the floor. What is left

but to make a world, a war?

Or a landscape in which to stay alive

(*ghost flower/ house of breath*). Another wish: language

drilled through ice, through my life.

If grief is love with nowhere to go, this is

my mouth turning into snow.

This is somewhere.

Camille Monet on Her Deathbed

after Claude Monet, oil on canvas, 1879

for Batyah

Daybreak through the glass world and after. / My mind is paper thin again. / Light rushing like water over her body. / This is the story I tell myself about time. / You have never been so quiet.

I don't want to be hospitalized. / A sentence giving in to itself, each word giving in. / *Monet painted his dead wife as the first sunlight was entering the room* (Heinrich). / I can see. / She has run out of pain completely.

This is the story I tell myself about death. / Looking through you like a keyhole. / One mirror held up to another to dig a tunnel through the mind. / I have crushed my pills with the back of a knife.

As if someone was digging in the snow to get to her, scraping the ice back with his fingers. / To get high and quiet my eyes. / I cannot stop looking at my book of paintings. / I cannot stop looking at you.

I lower my head and close one eye, as if looking through a microscope. / *Camille Monet on Her Deathbed* (47). / I must cut myself in half to see her. / To learn to die, she has closed both eyes and multiplied.

More blue-streaked yellow than light—her face threaded with white. / Like someone pulled underwater—I am trying to say one thing at a time. / Say one thing true. / I love you: / This is the story of my eyes.

Walk on the Cliff at Pourville

after Claude Monet, oil on canvas, 1882

after my aunt, who drove off Canyon Cliff and survived

Obsession is a form of movement, brushstroke, walking toward the cliff. Clouds painted where my eyes used to be. Once I watched a woman stand ankle deep in the ocean holding a microphone down to record the sound of water lapping, receding. So she can listen, I thought, whenever she wants. Forever. In the weather of my face, I have two questions. What is more violent than beauty? Will I ruin myself before you ruin me?

On the seventh day, I asked myself, What are you rowing toward? For instance, the sky is overlapping with my face. Or her face is painted over my face. I imagine one mouth blooming against another. Side by side, two women walk toward the cliff to see the ocean. Darkest blue inside green. My mother has one sister, I write, to add to the list of things that are true. I am trying to speak like water, like an oar moving through.

So loudly in the dream my throat is sore. There is nothing I can do. I am screaming through the thinking. Through the sound of thinking. It would be a mistake to say, she wrote in her notes, I'm without awe simply because I lack a God. How we cut eyeholes out of sheets to be ghosts for Halloween. I thought, A mouth hole to speak through. I speak through. I believe in the longing to believe in God. I believe in the longing for God.

I want to die and I want to see the ocean, and go home. The voicemail said, I'm not myself anymore. I don't know, I don't know. Who can tell the difference between the painted and actual soul? The eyes are canvas and oil. Once I hid behind a headboard as a child, got myself wedged so far behind no one could reach. I was an animal then. I am an animal now looking at a painting. Through every window in my mind, her mind.

Inside each horror, a sliver of awe. Underwater, the sound heightened and turned white. Smeared across my face. Just to be alive in the glass bottle of the mind. Do you see what I mean? Live on TV, her body airlifted from the car wedged on the rocks below. Once I glanced out a window to discover we were flying inside clouds, then just above them. If there was a moment of silence in my life, if there was a moment of clarity.

Walking toward the cliff, one woman opens a yellow parasol, listens to the other talk about the sky. Snow-white marbled blue. What is at stake is the mind. I am trying to think of another word for hospitalized. Inconsolable, the woman with the parasol replies. In the margins, I ask, What color is your anxiety? We must love one another or die, Auden wrote. And years later, revised: and die. We must listen to each other talk about the sky.

Acknowledgements

Thank you to the editors of the following, in which some of these poems first appeared:

"Description of Symptoms": Academy of American Poets' *Poem-a-Day*, selected by Diane Seuss

"Women in the Garden": *Guesthouse*

"Postcards to M.": *The Kenyon Review* and *Pushcart Prize XLVII: Best of the Small Presses*

"Walk on the Cliff at Pourville": Poetry Society of America's Lucille Medwick Memorial Award, selected by Cameron Awkward-Rich

"The Woman in a Green Dress" *ZYZZYVA*

Thank you to Four Way Books' Ryan Murphy and Martha Rhodes, who have continued to support my work for a decade. I remain tremendously grateful. You have made my writing life possible.

Thank you to Steve White, Jessica Treglia, Lorene Delany-Ullman, Scott Hulett, Colette LaBouff, Sara Berry, Collier Nogues, Chloe Honum, Hadara Bar-Nadav, Lisa Glatt, and David Hernandez, who have given me true company in this life. I love you.

Notes

Camille Monet was the first wife of Claude Monet, with whom she had two sons. She was the subject of many of his paintings, as well as the paintings of Renoir and Manet. At 32 years old, on September 5, 1879, she died in their home in Vétheuil, France. The cause of her death remains uncertain—possibilities include uterine cancer, tuberculosis, or an unsuccessful abortion.

Molly Brodak was a poet, memoirist, teacher, and baker. She was the author of two collections of poetry, *A Little Middle of the Night*, and *The Cipher*, as well as *Bandit: A Daughter's Memoir*, which explores her complex relationship with her father, who went to prison for robbing multiple banks. At 39 years old, on March 8, 2020, she took her life in the woods near her home in Atlanta, Georgia.

René Genovese was my dear and difficult friend for over twenty years. She worked in the field of mental health and substance abuse for most of her adult life. At 42 years old, on January 3, 2021, she took her life in her home in Petaluma, California.

Batyah White was my gentle, beautiful mother-in-law. She was married to my father-in-law for 37 years. At 66 years old, on December 15, 2021, she died of breast cancer at their home in Anaheim, California.

The wild green parrots described in "The Woman in a Green Dress" are a large population of green Amazons that pass through my neighborhood in California annually in late August and early September.

"Postcards to M" took inspiration from garden designer Itaru Sasaki's "Phone of the Wind." After his cousin was diagnosed with terminal cancer, Sasaki installed an old telephone booth in his garden in Otsuchi, Japan, so he could continue to speak with him posthumously.

"Description of Symptoms" was featured on Academy of American Poets' *Poem-a-Day* in 2023, which included an "About this Poem" section: "This poem was written after filling out medical intake forms for a doctor's appointment last year. I was grieving for a friend who had ended her life, and I was experiencing symptoms I could not quite articulate. The poem surprised me with its ending, reminding me that language is a place for love to go."

"Walk on the Cliff at Pourville" includes a sentence from poet Natalie Eilbert in her "About this Poem" section of the Academy of American Poets' *Poem-a-Day* series, for her poem "Afterlife." She writes, "It would be a mistake to say I am without awe simply because I lack a God—"

Monet: 1840–1926: Capturing the Ever-changing Face of Reality (TASCHEN, 2015), a hardcover monograph of Claude Monet's paintings by art critic and curator, Christoph Heinrich, was my chief source text in this collection, including direct quotes and paraphrases from art critics, and Heinrich himself. Images of the four Monet paintings I am in conversation with (*The Woman in a Green Dress, Women in the Garden, Camille Monet on Her Deathbed*, and *Walk on the Cliff at Pourville*) were viewed in this book, which remained open on my desk from March 2020 to March 2023.

Allison Benis White is the author of *The Wendys*, *Please Bury Me in This*, winner of the Rilke Prize, and *Small Porcelain Head*, selected by Claudia Rankine for the Levis Prize in Poetry. Her debut, *Self-Portrait with Crayon*, won the Cleveland State University Poetry Center First Book Prize. Her poems have appeared in *The American Poetry Review*, *The Kenyon Review*, *New England Review*, *Ploughshares*, *Pushcart Prize XLI & XLVII: Best of the Small Presses*, and elsewhere. She has received honors and awards from the Poetry Society of America, the San Francisco Foundation, and the Academy of American Poets. She teaches at the University of California, Riverside.

WE ARE ALSO GRATEFUL TO THOSE INDIVIDUALS WHO PARTICIPATED IN OUR BUILD A BOOK PROGRAM. THEY ARE:

Anonymous (14), Robert Abrams, Debra Allbery, Nancy Allen, Michael Ansara, Kathy Aponick, Jean Ball, Sally Ball, Jill Bialosky, Sophie Cabot Black, Laurel Blossom, Tommye Blount, Karen and David Blumenthal, Jonathan Blunk, Lee Briccetti, Jane Martha Brox, Mary Lou Buschi, Anthony Cappo, Carla and Steven Carlson, Robin Rosen Chang, Liza Charlesworth, Peter Coyote, Elinor Cramer, Kwame Dawes, Michael Anna de Armas, Brian Komei Dempster, Renko and Stuart Dempster, Matthew DeNichilo, Rosalynde Vas Dias, Patrick Donnelly, Charles R. Douthat, Lynn Emanuel, Blas Falconer, Laura Fjeld, Carolyn Forché, Helen Fremont and Donna Thagard, Debra Gitterman, Dorothy Tapper Goldman, Alison Granucci, Elizabeth T. Gray Jr., Naomi Guttman and Jonathan Mead, Jeffrey Harrison, KT Herr, Carlie Hoffman, Melissa Hotchkiss, Thomas and Autumn Howard, Catherine Hoyser, Elizabeth Jackson, Linda Susan Jackson, Jessica Jacobs, Deborah Jonas-Walsh, Jennifer Just, Voki Kalfayan, Maeve Kinkead, Victoria Korth, David Lee and Jamila Trindle, Rodney Terich Leonard, Howard Levy, Owen Lewis and Susan Ennis, Eve Linn, Matthew Lippman, Ralph and Mary Ann Lowen, Maja Lukic, Neal Lulofs, Anthony Lyons, Ricardo Alberto Maldonado, Trish Marshall, Donna Masini, Deborah McAlister, Carol Moldaw, Michael and Nancy Murphy, Kimberly Nunes, Matthew Olzmann and Vievee Francis, Veronica Patterson, Patrick Phillips, Robert Pinsky, Megan Pinto, Kevin Prufer, Anna Duke Reach, Paula Rhodes, Yoana Setzer, James Shalek, Soraya Shalforoosh, Peggy Shinner, Joan Silber, Jane Simon, Debra Spark, Donna Spruijt-Metz, Arlene Stang, Page Hill Starzinger, Catherine Stearns, Yerra Sugarman, Arthur Sze, Laurence Tancredi, Marjorie and Lew Tesser, Peter Turchi, Connie Voisine, Susan Walton, Martha Webster and Robert Fuentes, Calvin Wei, Allison Benis White, Lauren Yaffe, and Rolf Yngve.